Puberty

PreTeen Boys

Ages 9-12

Mara Lucas

Fist Printing, 2022
ISBN: 979-8-9864196-0-2
Little Griffin Press

Table of Contents

Introduction

Okay, promise me you won't freak out... it's time to talk about puberty. I know it seems weird, and you might even be a little bit (or a lot!) nervous about what happens to your body during this time. Puberty is totally normal, and everyone goes through it. This book will help prepare you for the changes you will experience, or maybe you have even noticed changes happening already. Either way, this book is a super useful guide to help answer questions you may have along the way!

Over the next several chapters, we will talk about the stages of puberty and things that will happen in your body over the next few years, like growth spurts, body odor, getting a deeper voice, and, yes, your private parts. We'll also talk about some important things like handling awkward social situations, recognizing bullying, and managing strong emotions. Puberty can feel like a puzzle with lots of different pieces, but this book is designed to help put them together so you can get a clear picture of what to expect as you go through it.

There's no way around it—you're going to experience lots of changes during puberty. Puberty can be a confusing time for boys, but you are not alone! Other kids have questions and may feel nervous too. Reading this book and learning what to expect during puberty will help you understand what's happening in your growing body, so you will be ready to handle it like a champ! Let's get started!

Chapter 1: So, What's Puberty Anyways?

In a nutshell, puberty is when you transition from being a boy to being a man. This is the time when hormones in your body cause changes that make your body grow and develop. These changes can affect everything from how tall you are to your appetite and reproductive system. Everyone goes through it, and it is totally normal. It can be a little overwhelming to think about all of the changes, but by the end of this book, you will know a lot about what to expect and what to do to take care of your body.

During puberty, your body will change and grow more and faster than at any other period in your entire life (except for when you were a little baby). These changes don't happen at once; they come in stages and can take several years. Every boy is unique, so puberty will be a bit different for everyone. You will go through puberty at your own pace, and that's totally okay!

We know these changes can feel kind of strange but remember that puberty is a normal part of life, and every boy (and girl) goes through it. So breathe; you are going to be okay!

When Does Puberty Start?

Boys usually begin puberty between ages 9 and 15. Although in some cases, puberty can begin as early as 8 years old and as late as 16. This big age range can explain why you or some of your friends may already be developing deeper voices and body hair while others still look and sound like little kids. This time can be a little frustrating for some boys who may notice their friends developing muscles or getting taller before they do. Everyone goes through puberty at a time that is right for their own body. So, if your friend is growing much faster than you, don't worry. You will grow too when your body is ready.

SIGNS OF PUBERTY

PHYSICAL

- Body Hair
- Body Odor
- Acne
- Muscle Increase
- Growth Spurt
- Voice Changes
- Penis and Testicle Growth

EMOTIONAL

- Mood Swings
- Bursts of Anger
- Sexual Thoughts
- Crushes

What Are the Stages of Puberty?

Puberty happens in 5 different stages in which your body will experience a variety of changes such as growth spurts, hair in new places, or new developments in your genitals or private parts. Every boy will go through each of these stages at their own pace. Let's take a look!

Stage 1

Stage 1 happens before you start to show any physical signs of puberty. This will be around age 9 or 10. At this time, your brain will begin to send signals to your body to prepare for upcoming changes. The hypothalamus and the pituitary gland begin to release hormones into your body. Hormones such as testosterone help your body grow and influence other changes such as your voice getting deeper or growing facial hair.

Stage 2

The physical signs of puberty will begin to show in Stage 2. This generally happens around age 11. You will probably notice that your testicles will start to get bigger. In addition, the skin that holds and protects the testicles (known as your scrotum) will also begin to get bigger. You may also see some pubic hair beginning to grow around the base of your penis.

Stage 3

In Stage 3, the physical changes become more noticeable. These changes are likely to begin around age 13. You'll go through a growth spurt where your height could increase roughly 2-3 inches per year. At this stage, you may notice that your muscles are getting larger, and your voice is changing and getting deeper. Your voice might even crack or squeak at times. As your voice box grows, your Adam's apple (a bump on the front of your throat) will become more noticeable too. Your testicles will continue to grow, and your penis will get longer. You may also start to have what's called nocturnal emissions, or wet dreams, at night when your body releases a sticky substance from your penis. Don't worry, it's normal!

Stage 4

Puberty will be in full blast now, and you'll be noticing some big changes. This stage usually begins around age 14. Some of the changes you are likely to see include your penis and testicles continuing to grow, and you might notice that your scrotum (the skin around your testicles) gets darker in color. You'll also begin to grow hair in your armpits, and you may even start to get acne (pimples). The voice change that started earlier will become a permanent deeper voice. These are all signs that your body is developing naturally.

Stage 5

This is the last stage of puberty, and you'll be reaching full physical maturity (fully developed), including your adult height. Stage 5 usually starts around age 15, and most boys reach full physical maturity by age 18. At this stage, you'll probably begin to grow facial hair and may need to start shaving. Your pubic hair will have fully grown out, and you may notice that it has spread to your inner thighs. Also, your penis and testicles will have reached adult size by the end of this stage.

Now that we have talked about the different stages of puberty and what to expect, hopefully, you are starting to feel a little more prepared for the changes you may be about to go through. Remember, puberty is a totally normal process that everyone goes through. Some boys may go through it early, and others might not experience it until later. Whatever happens, know that your body will go through puberty when it is ready and the time is right for you. Everyone's body is unique, and that includes you!

Each boy goes through puberty on their own timeline. It's important not to compare yourself to the other boys at school.

REMEMBER

Chapter 2: What's Happening to My Body?

One of the biggest things you are going to notice over the next couple of years is that your body will change. Everyone experiences these changes a little bit differently. Don't be alarmed if your friends start getting taller before you do or that one popular kid in your PE class has bulging biceps popping out of his T-shirt. You are unique, and your body will go through changes in its own way and at a pace that is right for you. It may not always be the pace you want, or you might not wake up with a superhero physique, but that is okay. Let's find out more about what changes you can expect.

Weird Science: Biology of Puberty

Genetics has to do with the building blocks that make up your body. Your unique body shape, height, weight, muscles, hair, and other factors are all influenced by your genes. Some boys notice huge changes that happen rapidly, while others might not notice as big of a difference, or they may experience changes more slowly. Everyone's body is different, and the types of changes can vary greatly. For example, some kids might experience a lot of acne, and some get very little. Some kids may gain a lot of muscle mass, but some don't see as much of a difference. Your biology and genetics play a big role in determining what types of changes your body will experience.

Another big factor is something called hormones. These are natural chemicals produced by your body that affect muscle growth, your voice, and other things. It's possible you've already heard about the hormone testosterone. During puberty, your body will begin to make testosterone rapidly, which leads to many of the changes you will experience during puberty, such as getting taller, stronger, and hairier. It is related to your reproductive system and can also make your voice change.

You know that kid with the very deep voice and the huge Adam's apple on his throat? He might have a lot of testosterone that caused those changes. Remember, everyone's body is different, so your voice might not be that deep, but it will change as your larynx and vocal cords grow. Sometimes your voice can go through a period where it sounds squeaky while your body goes through these changes. This can be both funny and embarrassing, but it's just something that's part of puberty that you and lots of other kids will go through.

You may also notice other changes as your body grows, such as a big change in your appetite. If your stomach is grumbling a bit more than usual, that is normal. You are at a time when your body is growing rapidly, and your metabolism is fired up. That means that your body may be burning calories much faster as it builds muscles and grows. Keep in mind that it is important to maintain a healthy diet. Just because your body is growing, that doesn't mean you should eat whatever you want all the time. Your body needs proper nutrients for healthy growth, which we will discuss more in Chapter 9.

The idea of growing muscles may sound exciting, but the changes you see might be very different from your friends or other kids. While you may dream of waking up to find that you have a superhero physique with jacked muscles, the reality is that the changes might not be that drastic. You might also find that your friend might get bigger muscles than you or have clearly defined ab muscles. While this can feel unfair, remember to accept that your body is unique and that your body will grow and change in the way that is right for you. If building a superhero body is your goal, you might want to start hitting the gym or working out because it might not happen on its own unless you get bitten by a radioactive spider or something.

My Clothes Don't Fit Again! Handling Growth Spurts

Many boys your age will experience something called a growth spurt. Typically, this happens between the ages of 10 and 15. This is a time when your body grows rapidly and could add up to around 4 inches or even more in a single year. That means you might find that you outgrow clothes more quickly than you used to. Growth spurts can also happen at different rates and at different times for you and your friends, so don't be surprised if one of them suddenly appears to be a bit taller when you see them after summer is over at the beginning of a new school year.

Growth spurts may sound cool because you get to grow tall really fast but hang on because there are a couple of other things you should know. The body typically grows disproportionately, so your hands and feet may grow first before your torso and legs, which can make you feel awkward or clumsy. Your chest and shoulders will get broader too, but it can take time for your whole body to finish growing and feel balanced again. Also, you might notice something called growing pains, which means your body can hurt due to all of the growing and stretching that is happening. It's normal, but if you feel a lot of pain, make sure you tell your parents or another adult so they can check in with a healthcare provider if needed.

Wait...Am I Going to Have to Start Shaving?

Maybe, but probably not right away. Don't worry; you probably won't wake up one morning with a giant beard on your face.

Although some kids might grow facial hair earlier than others, most boys will experience this usually around age 14 or 15. As you get older, you will start to notice hair growing in other areas too, such as your armpits, chest, back, legs, and pubic area.

Your hair might also start to feel more greasy as your skin produces something called sebum. This is an oily substance that your body creates to coat and protect your skin and hair. You will probably want to make sure you use a good shampoo and conditioner so your hair doesn't get too greasy. As you grow into a man, grooming is something you will want to pay more attention to for hygiene reasons and to maintain a positive self-image, which we will talk more about later. In the meantime, know that your body is going to change a lot in the next couple of years, and it can come with some pretty 'hairy' side effects.

Hairy Armpits, Smelly Socks, and Icky Pimples...Oh My!

While it can be neat to get taller and stronger, puberty can be a little bit...well, gross. As your body goes through so many changes, you also start to do things like sweat more when you play sports or exercise. This can cause stinky body odor or BO that other people might notice. Many boys your age start using something called deodorant to make sure they aren't smelly when they go to school or do other activities. Your clothes might also start to smell funky, so you will want to make sure you are doing laundry regularly and wearing clean clothes whenever possible.

Another common change is acne. Acne, or what you might know as pimples or zits, can form on your face and body. Some kids get lots of pimples, and others might not. This can be related to genetics, hormones, and also hygiene habits.

Pimples can be uncomfortable or even painful, so it is important to take good care of your skin. Making sure you wash your face to remove dirt and oils that can clog your pores is an important step. If you have more severe acne, talk with a parent or guardian to see what more you can do to help take care of it. For more serious acne, some kids may even go to a dermatologist or skin doctor for treatment recommendations.

All of these changes can be a bit overwhelming or even embarrassing. Unfortunately, there may be times when other kids might make rude comments or jokes about someone else by saying they smell bad or making fun of someone's appearance. This is not kind, and it can really hurt someone's feelings and self-esteem. Remember that everyone's body reacts a little bit differently during puberty, and it is important to be kind and respectful to others. We will also talk about things you can do if someone says or does something that bothers you in Chapter 10.

ACNE DO'S AND DON'TS

DO'S

- Get enough sleep
- Use a moisturizer
- Keep your face clean
- Avoid excessive stress
- Avoid greasy food
- Use ice to reduce swelling

DON'TS

- Use harsh products
- Touch your face exesively
- Pop or Squeeze your pimples
- Wash your face too often

Puberty Changes

e	d	v	t	a	o	q	z	v	b	o	i	m	s
z	u	m	o	o	d	s	w	i	n	g	s	z	w
i	u	t	p	a	s	a	h	g	b	a	c	i	u
h	e	i	g	h	t	p	m	a	f	d	f	t	v
u	y	m	u	s	c	l	e	s	v	s	y	h	q
p	i	o	n	n	e	r	g	e	a	i	u	j	e
w	t	f	j	g	e	h	r	r	k	p	n	f	r
r	r	y	a	c	n	e	p	j	o	q	p	g	m
k	i	b	i	o	l	o	g	y	d	w	e	l	m
n	d	e	o	d	o	r	a	n	t	y	i	v	e
b	o	d	y	o	d	o	r	x	k	u	f	n	i
q	p	d	o	x	j	a	r	m	p	i	t	s	g
o	i	l	y	o	h	o	r	m	o	n	e	s	t
p	x	q	x	f	p	i	m	p	l	e	s	s	q

ACNE
ARMPITS
BODY ODOR
GROWING
HORMONES
MUSCLES
SHAVING
ADAMS APPLE
BIOLOGY
DEODORANT
HEIGHT
MOOD SWINGS
PIMPLES

Chapter 3: Changes Down Under...

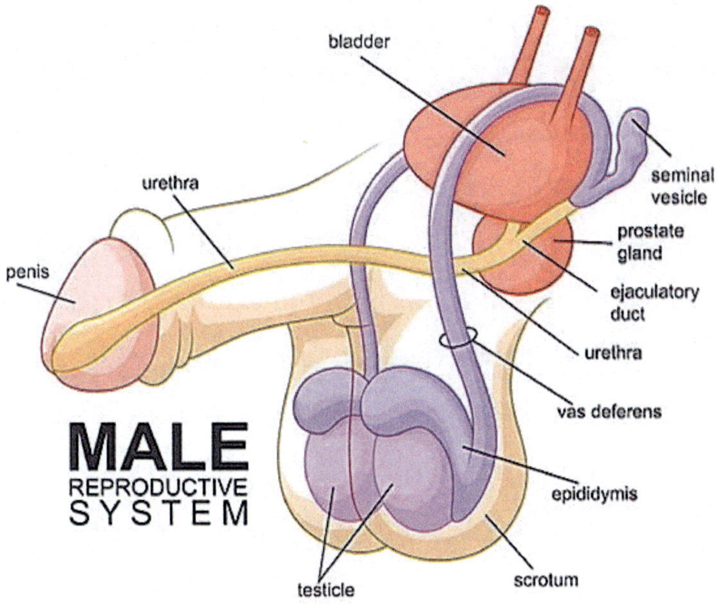

Going through puberty is no joke, and changes are happening all over your body. One of the biggest changes boys of your age will experience is changes in the genital area. Before we talk about the changes you can expect "down there," let's go over some anatomy.

Owner's Manual to Male Anatomy

The male body has a lot of unique...parts. You are likely familiar with many of them and how they operate, but let's do a quick overview. Your male anatomy is made up of a penis, scrotum, and testicles. This makes your biology different from females, who have other body parts. Some boys also have what is called the foreskin. This is a bit of extra skin at the end of your penis that is sometimes removed in a process called circumcision. Circumcision can vary depending on your culture or whatever your parents decided when you were born. Whether you are circumcised or not doesn't really matter much and is more of a religious, cultural, or personal preference. It does change the appearance of your penis, but it does not affect how it functions. If you are uncircumcised, the most important thing to keep in mind is that you need to do an extra good job keeping your penis clean, which we will discuss more in a later chapter.

Questions You Were Too Afraid to Ask

As a male, you might be wondering if your size is normal. The truth is most people have an average-sized penis. The size of your penis does not change how it functions, and it is okay if your body is different from others. Whether it is longer or smaller really does not matter as everyone's body is unique. Your penis works the same way as everyone else's and is the right size and shape for your body.

When you go through puberty, your genitals or private parts will experience some significant changes. Your penis will begin to grow longer, and your scrotum will also get bigger. You will also begin to grow what is known as pubic hair, or what you might hear some boys call 'pubes.' Your testicles will drop, meaning they will begin to rest lower in your scrotum and begin to prepare for reproduction. This means that your body is going to start going through changes that will prepare it for being able to make a baby. All of these changes are normal and an important part of the process of getting older.

The Incredible Male Reproductive System

As you go through puberty, your body's reproductive system will also develop. There are various changes your body will go through during this time, including the production of semen. This is a sticky substance that is released by the penis during a process called ejaculation. Semen contains millions of sperm, which can fertilize a female egg and result in a pregnancy and form a baby. If you thought storks dropped babies off on people's doorsteps, well, now you know that isn't exactly correct. But we'll discuss how babies are made a little more in-depth in chapter 5.

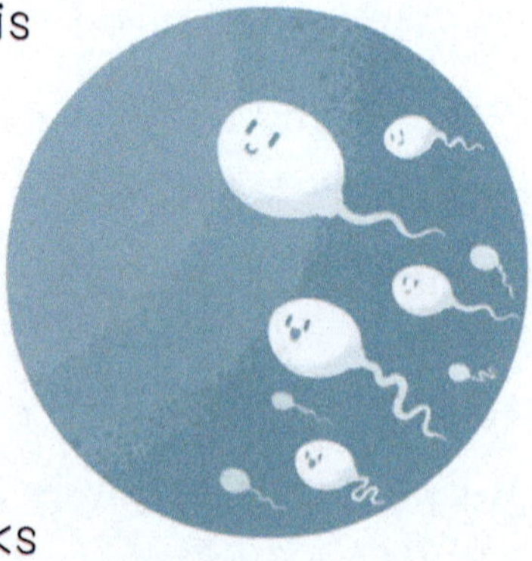

Many boys will experience a nocturnal emission, or what is sometimes referred to as a "wet dream." This means that you may experience an ejaculation while you are sleeping. This does not mean that you wet the bed or need to wear a diaper. Your body produces semen naturally, and sometimes it builds up and needs to be released. This is your body's natural way of releasing it.

These typically don't happen too often, but if you happen to wake up and find that you had a nocturnal emission, it might be a good idea to take a shower to clean up and make sure you also put on clean clothes. As you get older, nocturnal emissions tend to become less common and eventually stop altogether. It is also possible that you don't experience them at all, but if you do, now you know what is happening with your body.

Most adult males produce around 2 trillion sperm — that's 2 million million — in a lifetime! And even though it only takes one sperm to fertilize a female egg, the average ejaculation contains about 15 million sperm.

DID YOU KNOW?

MALE REPRODUCTIVE SYSTEM

Across

2. All boys are born with this extra skin to protect the tip of their penis.

5. This looks and works like a sac! Inside, it holds the testicles, which make sperm.

7. When your penis releases semen.

8. A tube that carries urine (pee) through the prostate and out of the penis.

9. When sperm enters the female ovum and creates a pregnancy.

Down:

1. It's about the size of a chestnut and produces some of the liquid that makes up semen.

3. This is when the foreskin is surgically removed, leaving the tip of the penis exposed.

4. This is a sticky substance called semen that is released by the penis during a process called ejaculation.

6. This collects urine until it's time for it to leave your body and lets you know when you gotta go to the bathroom.

Chapter 4: I Can't Fight This Feeling

Puberty brings about lots of new emotions and feelings that you may not be used to experiencing. On top of mood swings, you may start to feel some other intense emotions and bodily urges. While this may be a little alarming at first, it is a normal part of growing older that you need to be aware of and know how to handle.

I Don't Have a Crush on Them...Wait, Do I?

At this age in your life, lots of boys might start talking about 'liking' certain people or making jokes that you have a crush on someone. This is a totally normal part of growing up. You may feel romantic attraction to others as well as other strong emotions. Maybe it's the way their hair glistens in the sun, the deep beauty in their eyes, or their incredible personality. It

is very likely that you will develop a crush on someone at some point, or maybe you won't.

New Bodily Sensations and Urges

As your body develops, you may start to notice some different sensations or urges that you have not experienced before. This could be that your heart goes pitter-patter and beats a little faster when you see your crush. Along with this, your face might get red with embarrassment, or you might even get shaky with nervousness when you talk to someone you really like. You may also begin to feel physically attracted to someone in a way that you haven't felt before and begin to think about things like kissing, hugging, or even...sex.

Going through puberty means parts of your body, like your penis, may become a little more active. Sometimes boys may experience something called an erection, which is when their penis becomes hard. This can happen unexpectedly and be a bit embarrassing, but it is something that you may experience more frequently during puberty. It can also happen if you see someone you are attracted to. This is known as sexual arousal.

When people experience sexual arousal, they sometimes engage in sexual behavior. For some people, this might mean engaging in a private behavior called "masturbation" or "self-stimulation." Different families, cultures, and religions may have different guidelines or beliefs around this. You may wish to discuss this topic with a parent if you have questions or concerns about what is appropriate for you.

Stay In Your Lane: Respecting Boundaries

No matter what happens, there are a couple of important things to remember. Just because you like someone, it does not mean that you have to share how you feel or tell them. It also does not mean that you have to "go out" with anyone. While you might hear other kids talking about going out with or dating other people, it doesn't mean you have to do that. Right now, you might find it best to just focus on being friends and getting to know people better by starting a conversation, inviting them to sit at the same table at lunch, or offering to work together on a project.

While it is normal for you to develop a crush on someone or start to like someone, they might not feel the same way about you. It is important to make sure that you are aware of others' feelings and do not cross boundaries. For example, sitting too close to someone, staring at them, or making certain comments or gestures can make others feel very uncomfortable or even unsafe. It could also be considered inappropriate or even sexual harassment and get you in big trouble.

Your Body Your Say: Setting Boundaries

Always remember that your body belongs to you, and other people do not have the right to see or touch you, especially your private parts, without your permission or consent. You have the right to say what does and doesn't happen to your body. This doesn't mean you feel shame about your body or private parts, just that there are boundaries.

If you feel someone is behaving toward you in a way that makes you uncomfortable or unsafe or is doing something without your consent or permission, like an unwanted touch, you need to report it to a safe adult immediately to make sure it stops.

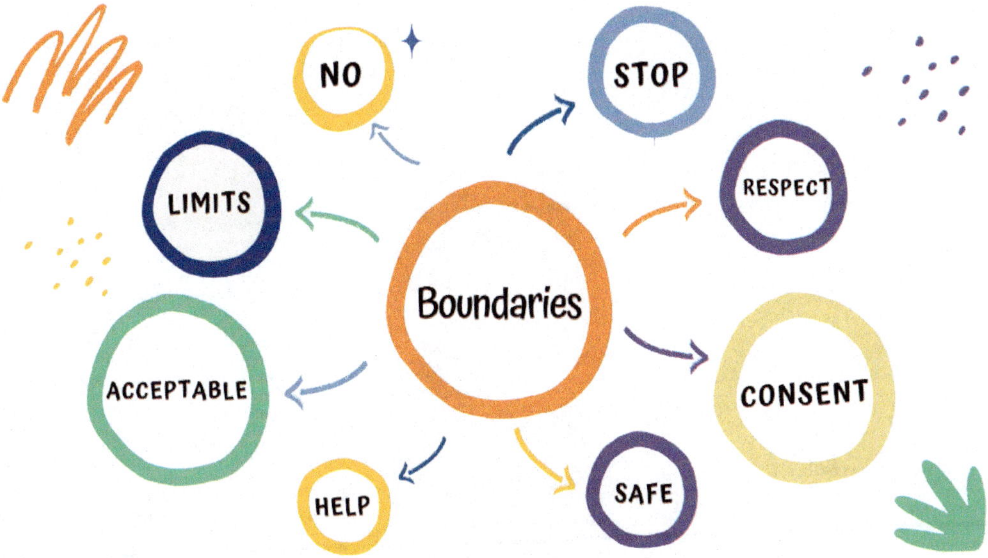

Personal Boundaries

Rules and limits you have for your body and how you want other people to treat you.

Chapter 5: So, What Is Sex?

Sex is a natural, healthy part of life. As you get older, you might start thinking about sex more. At some point, your body may start to react towards the person you like. You may feel strange new sensations when you see them, talk to them, or touch them, even if it's just their hand. This is called arousal and may result in an erection — or what some older boys may call a 'boner.' Although it may feel a bit embarrassing, it's perfectly normal. But just because you may have started thinking about sex and having feelings of arousal doesn't mean that you are mentally and emotionally ready to start having sex. While sex is natural and healthy, it's important to wait until you are mature enough to understand love and healthy relationships and the possible consequences of sex.

Why do people have sex?

There are various reasons why adults have sex. One of those reasons is to make a baby. Human beings want to reproduce, and one of the ways to do that is through sexual intercourse. During sex, a man inserts his penis into a woman's vagina and ejaculates semen containing sperm. The sperm may meet the woman's egg and fertilize it. The fertilized egg grows into an embryo and later a baby.

Making babies is not the only reason people have sex. Adults often kiss, hug, touch and engage in other sexual behaviors with one another to show caring for each other and to feel good. When it happens, the couple feels more connected to one another. Adults may also choose to have sex for pleasure. Sometimes adults look at pictures of naked people or people having sex on the internet, but this is not for kids. If you stumble across these images, you should turn it off or look away and talk to your parents or other trusted adult immediately. The when and why people choose to have sex really depends on their personal preferences, religion, and values.

A very important thing to remember is that sex should always be consensual. This means that both people want and agree to do it. Also, when you are mature enough to have sex, you'll want to practice safe sex. This means that you use a condom or other protection to prevent unwanted pregnancies or diseases.

But my friends are thinking about doing it...

As you go through puberty, your body will naturally grow and prepare for reproduction and sex. Talking about sex with your friends is normal, but this doesn't mean you should feel pressured to do it. At this stage, it's best to gather information and learn more about sex and relationships. Your friends probably won't know much at this age, so don't believe everything they tell you. Instead, talk to your parents or other trusted adult. It may be a little embarrassing, but they have your best interest at heart and will make sure you have the correct information.

Your parents especially know what is best for you and will do their best to not mislead you. They may want you to be a certain age or have certain experiences, such as a loving relationship before you have sex. This is because they love you and want you to be able to make responsible decisions for your future.

Sex and Physical Intimacy

My Parent's Values

Everyone has different values about sex and sexual intimacy. Talk to your parents about their values and expectations around sex and physical intimacy. How do you feel about it? Write about it below.

My Values

Take a moment to think about what your own values are. Write about it below.

Sex and Physical Intimacy

i	n	t	i	m	a	c	y	p	p	k	c	r	t
i	i	t	z	s	l	y	s	e	m	g	w	e	r
n	j	m	l	i	o	b	a	b	i	e	s	s	u
t	o	o	p	l	v	b	d	s	p	q	v	p	s
e	n	s	a	f	e	s	e	x	p	s	a	o	t
r	f	e	r	t	i	l	i	z	e	d	l	n	e
c	b	p	y	x	p	j	s	g	i	m	u	s	d
o	l	z	s	p	e	r	m	u	r	a	e	i	a
u	e	f	c	c	i	n	h	a	q	t	s	b	d
r	c	f	k	a	x	o	o	h	f	u	x	l	u
s	a	f	f	e	c	t	i	o	n	r	h	e	l
e	t	v	l	a	j	u	t	o	s	e	l	n	t
y	e	w	s	c	o	n	s	e	n	s	u	a	l
i	i	r	t	y	h	v	t	s	e	m	e	n	i

AFFECTION
CONSENSUAL
INTERCOURSE
LOVE
RESPONSIBLE
SEMEN
TRUSTED ADULT
BABIES
FERTILIZED
INTIMACY
MATURE
SAFE SEX
SPERM
VALUES

Chapter 6: Get Ready for Some Mood Swings!

As your body goes through puberty, your emotions are going to change a lot. This means that you might experience emotions that are very intense and change very quickly. This is common, but it is also something that you want to be prepared for so your emotions don't take you on a wild ride!

Paying Attention to Your Emotions

One of the most important skills in life is learning to recognize and manage your emotions. Whether you are dealing with your annoying little cousin, working on a difficult school project, or some other frustrating situation, strong emotions can get in the way and affect your decisions in negative ways. The first step in managing your emotions is being able to recognize what emotion you're experiencing. If you can't name how you are feeling, it can be difficult to handle it. During puberty, emotions can be a bit unpredictable, and they can zig-zag up and down and all over the place like a rollercoaster. Luckily, there are lots of ways to get better at recognizing your emotions and managing them.

An effective way to start recognizing your emotions better is to build your emotional vocabulary. Just knowing the names of different emotions can be a big help. Start keeping a list of the different emotions you experience or the emotions you come across in books you read or from other places like videos you've watched online. Another strategy is to pay attention to your body. Are you clenching your fists? Do you have butterflies in your stomach? Different responses in your body can be powerful clues to help you identify how you are feeling.

Is it Normal to Feel Like This?

Yes, it is normal to experience strong emotions and for them to change frequently at this age in your life. These rapid changes in emotions, such as going from happy to very angry, are called mood swings. This is caused by the changes your body goes through during puberty, such as your hormone levels changing, which can have a big impact on your emotions. Mood swings can be difficult to handle, but there are ways you can keep your cool the next time you feel a strong emotion like frustration, sadness, or even embarrassment.

How are you feeling?

happy

sad

bored

mad

scared

excited

playful

curious

tired

Take a Deep Breath, Dude! Handling Strong Emotions

Breathing is one of the most important things you can do when you have a strong emotion. When you get mad, nervous, or have another uncomfortable emotion, your body and brain may experience changes such as releasing a hormone called adrenaline or faster breathing. By taking the time to stop and breathe deeply a few times, you can help your body and brain start to calm down. Naming how you are feeling can also be helpful. As you calm strong emotions, it can also help you to focus better so that you make better decisions.

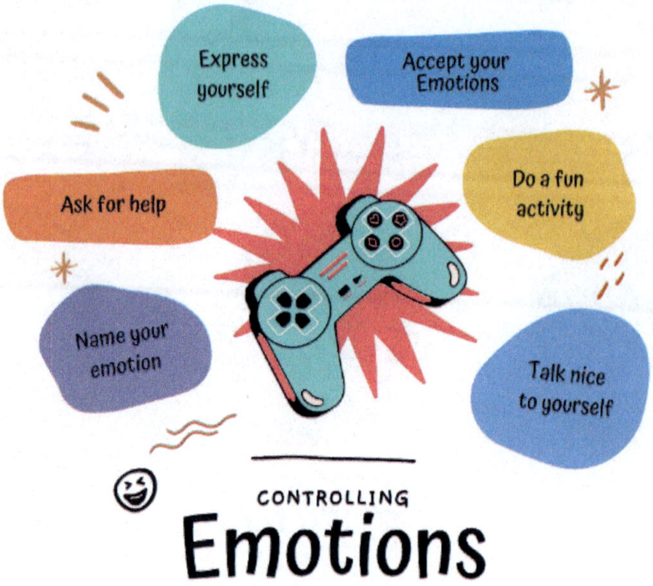

Using Positive Self-Talk

When we experience strong emotions like frustration because we missed a goal in soccer or embarrassment because we did something weird in front of our friends, we might start telling ourselves negative things like "I can't believe I did that!" or "I'm such an idiot." These comments are called negative self-talk, and they can hurt our self-esteem or impact our choices in negative ways.

It is okay to have strong emotions, but we need to be able to take a deep breath and use positive self-talk to help ourselves work through a difficult moment and be successful. Next time you make a mistake or are about to lose your temper because your locker won't open, remember to breathe and tell yourself something positive like "It's okay, I can do this" or "just relax."

What if I Need Help? It's Totally Fine to Get Help

Sometimes our emotions can be really strong and difficult to deal with. If you are having a hard time managing your emotions, it might be a good idea to ask an adult for help. You might feel embarrassed or like you are the only one who feels that way, but the truth is that many people need help with their emotions. Chances are you know at least one adult you could ask for help, such as a teacher, school counselor, family member, or even a coach. If you needed help with math, you would ask a teacher, right? The same thing is true for your emotions, and it's always okay to ask for help. Trust me, you're not the only boy that has strong emotions that are hard to deal with sometimes.

Moods and Emotions

l	n	e	r	v	o	u	s	w	t	e	u	o	r
v	x	q	r	z	u	e	o	m	a	w	m	d	o
s	u	r	p	r	i	s	e	d	f	a	e	i	i
m	r	c	z	u	c	k	l	r	r	h	z	s	v
g	f	h	c	f	s	a	d	c	a	o	o	g	m
r	b	e	u	r	b	o	u	s	i	p	s	u	t
u	f	e	r	m	o	h	r	t	d	e	c	s	p
m	a	r	i	w	n	a	g	r	g	f	a	t	w
p	n	f	o	n	i	p	u	m	y	u	r	e	o
y	g	u	u	j	c	p	c	s	l	l	e	d	r
g	r	l	s	b	j	y	a	q	s	e	d	i	r
i	y	r	g	r	a	t	e	f	u	l	k	q	i
m	p	j	e	a	l	o	u	s	o	m	f	k	e
q	m	d	a	m	h	e	w	u	m	l	b	j	d

AFRAID
CHEERFUL
DISGUSTED
GRUMPY
HOPEFUL
NERVOUS
SCARED
SURPRISED

ANGRY
CURIOUS
GRATEFUL
HAPPY
JEALOUS
SAD
SORRY
WORRIED

The Best Day of My Life

Think about what the best day of your life would be like. Write a story describing everything about that day. Why is is the best day ever?

Chapter 7: Man in the Mirror…Well, Almost

As you go through puberty, your body and appearance may change significantly. When you look in the mirror, you may start to notice changing facial features like a more defined jawline or skin changes such as acne. These changes can lead to a lot of emotions and affect how we feel about ourselves. While your appearance in the mirror may vary over the next couple of years, it is important to practice self-acceptance and maintain a positive self-image.

Ugh…Not Another Pimple! Learning to Accept Change

For some kids, acne can be hard to deal with. Nobody wants to go to class with a giant pimple on their nose, but it can happen sometimes. Remember that you are not the only kid with pimples. It is very common, and the important thing is to do what you can to take care of your skin. Again, pimples are commonly related to genetics, so there may not be a whole lot you can do about them. If they are bothersome or even painful, make sure you speak up about it and tell your parent or guardian. Depending on how serious they are, you may choose to use special skincare products or even talk to your doctor for support. As you take steps to be more accepting of your body, caring for your skin can help you feel more confident and build a positive self-image.

I Feel So Embarrassed! Situations that Affect Self-Esteem

Other changes in your body can be awkward too, such as feeling clumsy as your hands and feet grow at a different rate from the rest of your body or having your voice squeak in the middle of your science presentation. These situations can feel very embarrassing, but sometimes we need to learn to let things go and even see the humor in the situation. Being able to recognize that lots of kids go through the same stuff and that you're not alone can help you move forward and not let these situations affect your self-esteem too much. Your body is transitioning, and it is important to treat yourself with compassion and maintain a positive attitude.

Building a Positive Self-Image

There are other things that affect how you feel about yourself besides your appearance. This is a time of your life when you may be exploring lots of different activities and figuring out who you are. You may have changing interests in hobbies, music, fashion, friends, and lots of other things. Enjoy this time of exploring your interests and make an effort to be successful in goals that you set for yourself, like getting good grades or getting better at an activity you like. Surrounding yourself with positive people, being the kind of person you want to be, and putting energy towards things that are important to you can all help you build a positive self-image.

Many kids your age also worry about being popular or how many friends they have, but the most important thing is to enjoy being around friends you like spending time with and treating others with kindness. If you focus your energy on worrying about how popular you are, this might affect your self-esteem in a negative way as you could be comparing yourself with other people instead of being accepting of and confident in yourself. Instead of trying to be someone you are not to impress other people, just focus on being you. You are awesome.

Chapter 8: But...What if I'm Transgender?

Just because someone was assigned male at birth does not always mean this will be their gender identity as they get older. Some boys may be transgender and may not identify as being male. Instead, they may identify as being female, or they may be non-binary, meaning they do not identify as either male or female. This can make puberty—an already overwhelming stage—an even more confusing and challenging time. Let's talk about some things that may help make this time a little easier to navigate if you are transgender or are exploring this currently.

Gender Identity and Puberty

Gender identity is different from assigned sex at birth (male or female). People who identify as the same sex that they were assigned at birth are called cisgender. For example, if someone is born male, identifies as male and uses the pronouns he and him, they would be considered cisgender. If someone is assigned male at birth, but their gender expression is different, meaning that they identify as something else, this is referred to as transgender. For example, someone could be born male but identify as female and use the pronouns she and her. They might also identify as non-binary, neither male nor female, and use the pronouns they and them.

When it comes to puberty and body changes, this can be a very confusing time, and some kids may need support navigating this time. While their body may be doing things that are male in nature, this may contradict their gender expression and be uncomfortable or confusing. If you feel this way, it is okay and totally normal to have questions or to want support.

It's Okay to Ask: Questions Transgender Youth Have About Puberty

Going through puberty is already a confusing time for kids, and it can be even more so if you are transgender for different reasons. As your body goes through physical changes that do not match your gender identity, this can create anxiety and embarrassment. Sometimes transgender kids have not shared with others that they are transgender yet, and it can create even more stress and pressure and leave you wondering what steps to take next. If you are feeling anxious or worried about the changes happening in your body, it is important to ask an adult you trust. This may be a parent, teacher, school counselor, or another adult.

Many transgender students may have questions about things like which bathroom or locker room to use or what to do if other kids are not accepting of your identity or tease you. These are all important questions to ask, and it is important to speak up about your needs and tell a trusted adult such as a parent or your school principal if you have questions or concerns. There are many laws that protect gender inclusion to help make sure you feel safe.

You might also be wondering if there are medical options to support your affirmed gender identity. As medical science improves, some transgender individuals may choose to see a doctor called an endocrinologist that specializes in hormones. In some cases, they may prescribe a special medication commonly referred to as hormone or puberty blockers. This is a medicine that can suppress the effects of puberty, which some transgender or gender-diverse patients may find helpful.

Speaking Up and Getting Support

If you are feeling concerned about puberty or have questions, you are not alone. Whether you are transgender or not, everyone's puberty journey is unique, and there are no right or wrong questions. Keeping all of your questions and strong emotions like anxiety inside can be unhealthy and lead to mental health concerns. Identify a safe and trusted adult that you can go to for support and let them know what you are going through. There are lots of people who care and can connect you with the right resources and support.

Diversity and Inclusion

r	s	t	e	r	e	o	t	y	p	e	c	j	v
p	u	t	b	s	m	x	t	u	z	h	i	y	p
e	c	h	n	p	t	i	o	s	m	e	s	d	o
r	r	z	z	o	t	y	s	t	c	v	g	i	b
s	j	x	p	n	n	e	b	n	w	y	e	v	i
o	d	u	e	r	n	b	a	y	h	i	n	e	n
n	g	d	d	r	e	t	i	y	v	q	d	r	c
a	i	e	i	g	p	j	b	n	o	l	e	s	l
l	g	a	n	e	m	f	u	m	a	j	r	i	u
i	f	v	c	d	f	e	z	d	a	r	t	t	s
t	x	c	l	j	e	h	n	s	i	h	y	y	i
y	a	v	v	k	m	r	s	t	l	c	p	w	o
u	e	q	u	a	l	i	t	y	z	o	e	l	n
l	h	q	x	r	c	u	l	t	u	r	e	i	o

ACCEPTANCE
CULTURE
EQUALITY
GENDER
INCLUSION
NONBINARY
PREJUDICE
CISGENDER
DIVERSITY
FAIRNESS
IDENTITY
JUDGMENT
PERSONALITY
STEREOTYPE

Chapter 9: Taking Care of Your New Body

As you start to grow and change during puberty, it is important to take good care of your body. Rapid changes mean there will be a lot of things to keep track of and maintain, such as good hygiene and eating properly to make sure your body is well taken care of.

What is That Awful Smell? Oh, It's Just Me Again

One of the biggest drawbacks of puberty is getting body odor. Nobody wants to be the stinky, sweaty kid in class. Being smelly can be embarrassing and gross other kids out. Be aware of your own body and be proactive. At a minimum, you need to make sure you are taking a shower regularly and wearing clean clothes whenever possible. It is especially important to wear

clean socks and underwear, as well as making sure that you wash clothes that are sweaty or smelly from PE or playing sports. Not cleaning clothes can actually lead to bacteria and fungal growth and other germs that can make you sick or cause skin problems like athlete's foot and jock itch.

Many kids your age also start to wear deodorant so they smell a little bit fresher. Some kids your age might discover body sprays or other fragrances and think these smells might make them more attractive; however, too much can actually have the opposite effect and be bothersome. Don't overdo it. Using different grooming products such as fragrances, hair gel, or deodorants can be a great way to maintain a clean appearance and improve your self-image, but do so in moderation.

There are other aspects of personal hygiene that you need to take note of also. Things like excessive ear wax, nose hairs, or dirty fingernails can be unsightly and gross out your classmates. You also need to make sure you wash your private area and armpits well, as these areas can get especially smelly. If you are uncircumcised, take extra care to pull back your foreskin and clean your private area well. If you don't, bacteria and a sticky substance called smegma can accumulate underneath and create serious skin problems that could even require circumcision. If that sounds painful, you are probably right. Take care of your body and keep it clean. Seriously.

"Hey, Go to Bed! I'm Trying to Grow!" Sincerely, Your Body

As you get older, your body needs adequate sleep. Most of your body's growth actually happens while you are asleep, so it is really important to make sure you are going to bed at a reasonable time. During puberty, your body needs around nine hours of sleep every night to rest, recover, and grow. If you stay up until midnight playing video games and then wake up at 7:00 a.m. every morning, you are not getting enough sleep. Lack of sleep can start to affect your body in negative ways and even make you less focused at school.

Optimize your body's growth and wake up ready for your day by making sure you go to bed on time every night. Getting enough sleep will help your body grow properly and give you the energy you need for your busy schedule, such as going to school and soccer practice. Being well-rested will also help you concentrate in class and keep your grades up. Make sure that sleep is a priority and that you go to bed on time. Maintaining a consistent sleep routine is one of the best ways to take care of your body as you go through puberty.

Staying Active: Putting Your New Body to Work

Another important aspect of puberty is moving your new body. As your muscles develop and your body grows, you need to put it to work with regular exercise. Whether it's playing basketball, walking the dog, or doing pushups in your bedroom, find ways to stay active. As your limbs grow and your muscles change, putting them to use will help you improve your coordination and establish better control of your body. This helps you get used to your new body and can also provide other health benefits such as releasing stress. So, put down the video game controller once in a while and go for a bike ride or do something active to get more than just your thumbs moving.

Did You Eat All of the Chips Again? Getting Proper Nutrients

During puberty, your appetite may increase. In fact, you may be hungry a lot because your body could be going through a growth spurt and need lots of energy to grow. Just because you are hungry doesn't mean you should eat everything in sight, though. While your metabolism may be in high gear, it can feel like you can eat whatever you want and you just keep growing, but your body needs certain vitamins and nutrients. Think of food as the fuel you put in your body to help it grow, and make sure you don't just fill up on junk food and sugary sodas. Eating a healthy diet is important for optimal growth and body performance.

Eating nothing but chips and cookies might not be the best strategy if you want to make the varsity wrestling team or improve your mile time. Everyone's body and nutritional needs are different, but in general, most kids need a variety of healthy fruits and vegetables, lean proteins, and quality carbohydrate sources. If you have questions about what to eat, talk to your parent or guardian to see if you can figure out a plan that works best for your body. Building healthy nutrition habits that you can carry with you as you get older is a great way to build a strong foundation for a lifetime of good health.

PERSONAL HYGIENE

Across:

1. I should do this every day to remove food from between my teeth
3. This is what I use to groom or style my hair.
6. I need to change this at least once a day to keep my private parts fresh.
8. I do this before I eat, after using the bathroom, sneezing, or playing with pets.
9. I use this to wash my body and my hands.
10. I trim these every week and keep them short and clean.

Down:

2. It's important that I do this every day to keep clean and smell fresh, especially after sports practice or playing outside.
4. I do this regularly to prevent bad breath, gingivitis, and cavities.
5. I clean these regularly to remove excess wax.
7. This gets applied to the armpits to control sweat and body odor.

Smelling Fresh

k	j	i	z	j	t	y	k	n	r	h	r	v	t
t	a	z	p	p	q	w	y	e	k	w	u	y	o
l	c	l	e	a	n	s	w	x	k	s	e	o	o
a	z	g	e	k	w	o	r	t	s	o	h	n	t
u	u	v	y	p	h	r	n	o	o	s	v	m	h
n	n	x	v	s	u	a	l	p	a	x	d	y	b
d	d	u	k	c	r	f	m	w	f	d	t	t	r
r	e	x	x	o	s	a	h	v	s	o	a	p	u
y	r	i	d	y	h	t	p	t	o	w	e	l	s
c	w	o	u	s	u	d	r	q	a	m	w	s	h
z	e	h	m	o	e	v	b	a	t	h	i	n	g
d	a	y	m	b	o	d	y	w	a	s	h	e	z
v	r	b	a	c	t	e	r	i	a	r	t	c	p
l	d	n	b	o	d	y	s	p	r	a	y	d	j

BACTERIA
BODY WASH
CLEAN
FLOSS
MOUTHWASH
SHOWER
TOOTHBRUSH
UNDERWEAR

BATHING
BODYSPRAY
DEODORANT
LAUNDRY
SHAMPOO
SOAP
TOWEL

Chapter 10: What if They Laugh at Me?

As you go through puberty, you are going to feel different. This might be even harder if you go through these changes before or after your friends do. Sometimes other kids make mean jokes or say things that can bother you. As you navigate all of these changes, it is important to know what to do if you run into problems with your peers.

I Feel Different from Everyone Else

Puberty can make you feel weird. It's okay; other kids feel weird too. Puberty is a huge transition in your life, and you are going through a lot of new experiences. Your emotions can be all over the place, your shoes don't fit, and you get pimples in the worst possible places. Puberty can be embarrassing, confusing, and tough. To make it even harder, someone might make fun of you or laugh at you. This is not fun to deal with, and it is important to know what to do if you are in a situation where you feel uncomfortable or need support.

Other People Keep Teasing Me: Handling Problems

Situations can come up where someone says or does something that bothers you or makes you feel bad. If other kids make jokes or put you down in some way, it's important to have some strategies to help deal with these problems. For some kids, this means speaking up and using a strong and respectful voice to ask them to stop. Often kids are just joking and don't realize that it really bothers you. If you let them know you want them to stop using a serious and assertive voice, usually they will get the message and leave you alone. Assertiveness is being able to stick up for yourself in a respectful way. It does not mean being rude back to the other person.

Other times you might try other strategies like ignoring their rude comments and choosing not to be around them. When someone says something rude or mean, sometimes you may feel like responding with a rude comment of your own to get back at them. Doing this only escalates the problem and can actually turn a one-sided bullying situation into a two-sided conflict.

That means you could be just as likely as the other person to get in trouble because you are both being mean even though they may have started it. Be careful to make a wise choice if you are in a situation where someone else has said something that bothers you.

If someone says or does something that really upsets you, you might need to take some time to cool off, so you don't say or do anything back that just makes the problem worse. Remember when we talked about mood swings? Your emotions can change very quickly, and you don't want to lose your temper and do something you will later regret. If you notice that you are getting angry, stop and take a deep breath, walk away, or use another strategy to help yourself get calm and handle the situation in an appropriate and respectful way.

What if They Don't Stop? Recognizing Bullying

If you have tried telling someone to stop or talking it out with them, but the problem is not getting better, you need to report it. If a problem continues to happen, it can turn into a serious situation called bullying. Bullying is when someone continues to treat someone else in a mean way without stopping. There are different types of bullying to be aware of. One common type of bullying is verbal. This is when someone says mean, hurtful words, such as making fun of someone's appearance or their body in some way. Everyone's body is different, and it is important to make sure that you do not make rude comments about another person in this way.

Another type of bullying is called cyberbullying. This could include being mean online such as sending a rude email or mean text messages. Cyberbullying is serious and can be even worse than in-person bullying because messages can be sent to a large group of people very quickly. Another type of bullying is physical. Pushing, hitting, or tripping someone can be very unsafe.

Bullying is serious and needs to be reported immediately. If it is not reported, it could keep happening or get worse. It could also spread, and other kids might be getting picked on or made fun of too. No matter if bullying is happening on the bus, in the lunchroom, or somewhere else, don't wait to report it. Speaking up and telling an adult what is going on can help to make sure that the problem stops.

Reporting and Getting Help

If you feel like bullying is happening, it needs to be reported right away to a teacher, bus driver, parent, or another adult. This could be a situation where you have tried asking someone to stop multiple times, but it keeps happening, or it could be a situation where someone did something unsafe like pushing or hitting someone. If something is ever unsafe, you need to make sure you report it immediately. It is not tattling;

it is being a responsible reporter and doing the right thing to get help and keep yourself and others safe.

In some cases, kids are scared to report what is happening because they are afraid that someone will find out that they told on them. They worry that if they find out they reported them, they will be even more mean, and the situation will get worse. This is usually not true. In fact, when kids report bullying, adults can get involved to help make sure that everyone is safe and work with the person who is doing the bullying to help them change their behavior and make more positive choices.

Sometimes you might find yourself in a situation where you witness someone being mean to another person. This is called being a bystander. If you are a bystander, there are different ways that you can help, such as by telling the person bullying to stop if you feel comfortable doing so or going straight to an adult to report it. You can also help stop bullying situations by making sure other kids are included or by being a friend to the person that was being picked on. Kindness and reporting are two of the best ways to help make sure bullying is prevented.

Chapter 11: Just Ask – Talking with Parents and Other Adults

As you have probably figured out by now, puberty is going to be a time of lots of changes. You are likely to have lots of questions during this time, and you might feel a little strange or embarrassed talking about things like private parts or having a crush on someone and not knowing what to do about it. Puberty can be very uncomfortable for a lot of kids, but you are not alone. Other kids experience similar feelings and often have the same kinds of questions you do. So, just ask! There are no questions that are too weird or too embarrassing to ask. The important thing is to get your questions answered so you don't feel confused or anxious.

It's Okay if You Feel Weird...Relax, You're Normal

You are normal. Your body is doing some new, and maybe a little weird, stuff that you are not used to, but it is a regular part of growing older. It is okay to feel concerned or worried about different things like growing hair in new territories or handling having a crush on someone for the first time. If you are not sure about something or have a question, ask an adult you trust. Sure, it might be a little bit embarrassing to ask, but it's important to be honest and open with someone about what you're feeling and going through. Puberty can be overwhelming, and you need to have someone to go to for support.

Who Do You Feel Comfortable Talking To?

Think about all the people in your life that care about you. Whether it is a parent, teacher, or even an older sibling, identify someone you feel comfortable talking with if you have questions about the changes you are experiencing. You don't have to go through puberty alone. Keeping questions and concerns to yourself can make you feel even more anxious or confused, so it is best to talk to someone you know if you need help with something. Who do you feel most comfortable talking to?

Some kids find it helpful to make a list of these different individuals. Maybe it's your school counselor, baseball coach, or even your big brother. These people are part of what can be considered your support system. A support system is a group of people you can rely on if you have questions or need help with something. Whether you have questions about puberty or other things like handling friendship problems, you want to make sure that you have a few people that you feel confident going to for assistance.

Seriously, Just Ask...Adults Have All Been Through Puberty

Puberty can feel really awkward, and you might be scared to ask, but don't be. There is no question you can't ask. Adults have all been through puberty too, so they can probably relate to how you are feeling. When they went through puberty, they might have had many of the same questions and concerns that you have. If they aren't sure how to help, they may be able to help you find the right person who can. For some kids, talking to their parents might feel uncomfortable, so you may want to talk with someone at school or maybe even an older brother or cousin who has been through puberty.

While most adults will be glad to answer your questions and help, if you feel like you don't get the support you need, don't give up. Sometimes adults might not be sure what to say or can feel uncomfortable talking about certain topics. If this is the case, think of another adult to talk with, such as a teacher. The important thing is to keep seeking the support you need and to advocate or speak up for yourself. Advocating for yourself means that if you need help with something that you recognize that your needs are important, you take them seriously, and you seek support.

Conclusion

Puberty is a normal part of growing up. Everyone's journey through puberty is unique, and there will be pros and cons, or things you like and things you don't. There may be strange or uncomfortable things, like having your voice change or getting acne, but you may also find that there are benefits such as getting taller or more muscular. Whatever your experience is, remember that your body is going through the changes that are right for you. Whether you go through puberty before your friends or after, your body is changing at the time that is right for you too.

In the next few years, you are going to start transitioning from being a child into the person you will be as an adult. This is a very important period in your life, and there are going to be times when it is hard or confusing. Make sure that you know who your support system is if you have questions or need help navigating things. Stay positive and enjoy the ride!

Puzzle Solutions

Puberty Changes - Solution

e	d	v	t	a	o	q	z	v	b	o	i	m	s
z	u	m	o	o	d	s	w	i	n	g	s	z	w
i	u	t	p	a	s	a	h	g	b	a	c	i	u
h	e	i	g	h	t	p	m	a	f	d	f	t	v
u	y	m	u	s	c	l	e	s	v	s	y	h	q
p	i	o	n	n	e	r	g	e	a	i	u	j	e
w	t	f	j	g	e	h	r	r	k	p	n	f	r
r	r	y	a	c	n	e	p	j	o	q	p	g	m
k	i	b	i	o	l	o	g	y	d	w	e	l	m
n	d	e	o	d	o	r	a	n	t	y	i	v	e
b	o	d	y	o	d	o	r	x	k	u	f	n	i
q	p	d	o	x	j	a	r	m	p	i	t	s	g
o	i	l	y	o	h	o	r	m	o	n	e	s	t
p	x	q	x	f	p	i	m	p	l	e	s	s	q

Sex and Physical Intimacy - Solution

i	n	t	i	m	a	c	y	p	p	k	c	r	t
i	i	t	z	s	l	y	s	e	m	g	w	e	r
n	j	m	l	i	o	b	a	b	i	e	s	s	u
t	o	o	p	l	v	b	d	s	p	q	v	p	s
e	n	s	a	f	e	s	e	x	p	s	a	o	t
r	f	e	r	t	i	l	i	z	e	d	l	n	e
c	b	p	y	x	p	j	s	g	i	m	u	s	d
o	l	z	s	p	e	r	m	u	r	a	e	i	a
u	e	f	c	c	i	n	h	a	q	t	s	b	d
r	c	f	k	a	x	o	o	h	f	u	x	l	u
s	a	f	f	e	c	t	i	o	n	r	h	e	l
e	t	v	l	a	j	u	t	o	s	e	l	n	t
y	e	w	s	c	o	n	s	e	n	s	u	a	l
i	i	r	t	y	h	v	t	s	e	m	e	n	i

Moods and Emotions - Solution

l	n	e	r	v	o	u	s	w	t	e	u	o	r
v	x	q	r	z	u	e	o	m	a	w	m	d	o
s	u	r	p	r	i	s	e	d	f	a	e	i	i
m	r	c	z	u	c	k	l	r	r	h	z	s	v
g	f	h	c	f	s	a	d	c	a	o	o	g	m
r	b	e	u	r	b	o	u	s	i	p	s	u	t
u	f	e	r	m	o	h	r	t	d	e	c	s	p
m	a	r	i	w	n	a	g	r	g	f	a	t	w
p	n	f	o	n	i	p	u	m	y	u	r	e	o
y	g	u	u	j	c	p	c	s	l	l	e	d	r
g	r	l	s	b	j	y	a	q	s	e	d	i	r
i	y	r	g	r	a	t	e	f	u	l	k	q	i
m	p	j	e	a	l	o	u	s	o	m	f	k	e
q	m	d	a	m	h	e	w	u	m	l	b	j	d

MALE REPRODUCTIVE SYSTEM

Across

2. All boys are born with this extra skin to protect the tip of their penis.

5. This looks and works like a sac! Inside, it holds the testicles, which make sperm.

7. When your penis releases semen.

8. A tube that carries urine (pee) through the prostate and out of the penis.

9. When sperm enters the female ovum and creates a pregnancy.

Down:

1. It's about the size of a chestnut and produces some of the liquid that makes up semen.

3. This is when the foreskin is surgically removed, leaving the tip of the penis exposed.

4. This is a sticky substance called semen that is released by the penis during a process called ejaculation.

6. This collects urine until it's time for it to leave your body and lets you know when you gotta go to the bathroom.

Diversity and Inclusion - Solution

r	s	t	e	r	e	o	t	y	p	e	c	j	v
p	u	t	b	s	m	x	t	u	z	h	i	y	p
e	c	h	n	p	t	i	o	s	m	e	s	d	o
r	r	z	z	o	t	y	s	t	c	v	g	i	b
s	j	x	p	n	n	e	b	n	w	y	e	v	i
o	d	u	e	r	n	b	a	y	h	i	n	e	n
n	g	d	d	r	e	t	i	y	v	q	d	r	c
a	i	e	i	g	p	j	b	n	o	l	e	s	l
l	g	a	n	e	m	f	u	m	a	j	r	i	u
i	f	v	c	d	f	e	z	d	a	r	t	t	s
t	x	c	l	j	e	h	n	s	i	h	y	y	i
y	a	v	v	k	m	r	s	t	l	c	p	w	o
u	e	q	u	a	l	i	t	y	z	o	e	l	n
l	h	q	x	r	c	u	l	t	u	r	e	i	o

Boundaries - Solution

o	g	d	f	g	m	i	e	e	l	j	i	t	c
o	t	z	u	g	p	t	z	a	p	y	z	f	s
v	f	x	i	y	c	x	c	r	h	k	s	w	g
c	k	w	o	e	w	i	k	t	i	t	a	w	k
m	k	d	p	k	s	c	l	u	i	q	d	s	e
l	c	s	l	y	a	a	j	m	e	n	p	o	m
j	e	j	h	a	e	y	i	o	q	i	f	e	o
r	s	p	g	h	c	l	k	h	o	w	v	c	t
m	t	l	e	r	f	r	u	a	c	s	x	o	i
y	o	t	o	f	b	c	q	g	d	a	h	n	o
l	p	s	p	a	c	e	o	g	c	f	t	s	n
m	e	p	e	x	o	n	t	p	m	e	y	e	a
f	f	p	e	r	s	o	n	a	l	t	i	n	l
c	k	z	m	l	d	z	b	v	g	y	b	t	z

PERSONAL HYGIENE

Across:

1. I should do this every day to remove food from between my teeth
3. This is what I use to groom or style my hair.
6. I need to change this at least once a day to keep my private parts fresh.
8. I do this before I eat, after using the bathroom, sneezing, or playing with pets.
9. I use this to wash my body and my hands.
10. I trim these every week and keep them short and clean.

Down:

2. It's important that I do this every day to keep clean and smell fresh, especially after sports practice or playing outside.
4. I do this regularly to prevent bad breath, gingivitis, and cavities.
5. I clean these regularly to remove excess wax.
7. This gets applied to the armpits to control sweat and body odor.

Thank You for Reading This Book

I would love to hear what you thought of the book.

Please take two minutes to leave your honest review on Amazon. Your helpful feedback will be greatly appreciated by other potential readers and me.

Thanks so much!

Mara Lucas

Glossary

Abstinence: Choosing to avoid doing certain sexual behaviors for a period of time.

Acne: Pimples that form on your face and body.

Adolescence: The transitional period after the start of puberty during which a person develops from a child to an adult.

Bladder: The sac that holds urine (pee) until you're ready to expel it (go to the bathroom)

Body Image: This is how you feel in your own body, including how you feel about your appearance.

Body Odor: Strong or unusual smell on the body usually caused by excessive sweating

Boundaries: Limits and rules that we set for ourselves in our interactions with others. They define what behaviors are acceptable and not acceptable to us.

Bullying: Intimidating or physically harming another person. This is often done repeatedly and can be in person or through technology such as social media.

Circumcision: When the foreskin is surgically removed, leaving the tip of the penis exposed. Some parents choose to circumcise their child based on personal, cultural, or religious beliefs.

Cisgender: Someone that identifies with the sex assigned to them at birth.

Consent: Giving permission for someone to touch you or take other action towards you.

Consensual: When something is done with the agreement or consent of both parties

Cyberbullying: Bullying someone online by sending or posting negative, hurtful, false, or mean content about someone else.

Ejaculation: When your penis releases semen.

Erection: When the penis becomes hard because of increased blood flow.

Epididymis: A narrow tube attached to each testicle where sperm cells are stored.

Fertilization: When sperm enters the female ovum (egg) and creates a pregnancy. This is also called conception.

Foreskin: A protective covering over the tip of the penis. All boys are born with a foreskin; however, in some boys, this skin has been removed through a process called circumcision.

Gender Identity: A person's sense of who they are — male, female, neither, or both.

Genitals: Another word for your private parts. This includes your penis, scrotum, and testicles.

Growing Pains: When your body hurts because it is growing a lot.

Growth Spurt: An increase in weight and height and other body changes that happen as kids get older.

Heterosexual: People who are attracted to people from the opposite sex.

Hormone: A natural chemical that controls different processes in your body.

Hypothalamus:	The part of the brain that controls body temperature, hunger, thirst, mood, and sex drive.
Intimacy:	The physical or emotional closeness you feel with another person.
Larynx:	An organ in the neck involved in sound and breathing. It is also known as the voice box.
Masturbation:	Self-stimulation or touching the genital area to the point of arousal.
Metabolism:	The chemical process in the body's cells that change food we eat into energy for the body.
Mood Swings:	A sudden and intense change in emotions, for example, going from feeling happy to sad very quickly.
Nocturnal Emissions:	When your body ejaculates while you are sleeping — also called wet dreams.
Penis:	An external male reproductive organ that carries semen and urine outside of the body. It is made from erectile tissue

Pituitary:	A small organ in the brain that produces hormones that control growth and development
Prostate:	A small gland located just below the bladder that helps produce semen.
Puberty:	The process of growing that includes changes to your body and reproductive system.
Pubic Hair:	Hair that grows in your private area during puberty.
Reproductive System:	The system of organs and glands involved in procreation or the creation of new life (children)
Safe Sex:	Sexual activity in which people take precautions to protect themselves against unwanted pregnancies and sexually transmitted diseases.
Scrotum:	The bag of skin that holds the testicles
Sebum:	An oily substance produced by the body that coats and protects the skin.

Self-Esteem:	How you feel about yourself. Having good self-esteem means you mostly feel good about yourself.
Semen:	A sticky substance created by the male reproductive system that contains sperm.
Seminal Vesicle:	The glands that produce the fluids that turn into semen
Sex Assigned at Birth:	It is the sex label (male or female) assigned to a person when they are born, most often based on the external anatomy.
Sex Hormones:	The chemicals produced by the body that control the growth of reproductive organs and sexual characteristics in the body.
Sex Positive:	Promoting an open and tolerant attitude towards sex and sexuality.
Sexual Abuse:	Any sexual touch or activity where consent (permission) has not been given. All sexual contact between an adult and child, whether permission has been given or not, is sexual abuse.

Sexual Intercourse: Sexual contact between two people involving penetration of a person's genitals into another

Sperm: The male reproductive cell which enters the female during sexual intercourse to penetrate and fertilize the egg.

Testicles: Two small oval-shaped organs (also called testes) found inside the scrotum. They make and store sperm cells and produce the sex hormone testosterone.

Testosterone: A male sex hormone mainly produced in the testes and plays a role in growth, reproduction, and development of male sexual characteristics.

Transgender: When an individual identifies as a gender different from their assigned sex at birth.

Trusted Adult: This is a person you trust and feel safe with because you feel they have your best interest at heart.

Urethra: A tube that carries urine (pee) through the prostate and out of the penis. It also carries semen from the testes out of the body

Vagina: The internal part of a women's genitals that receives the penis during sex and serves as the birth canal during childbirth. It is where babies come out.

Values: The things that are important to you in life.

Vas Deference: The tubes that carry sperm out of the testes in anticipation of ejaculation

Wet Dreams: When your body ejaculates while you are sleeping — also called nocturnal emissions.

Resources and Further Reading

Amaze
Taking the awkward out of sex ed.
https://amaze.org/

Committee For Children
Bullying Prevention Resources
https://www.cfchildren.org/resources/bullying-prevention-resources/

Every Body Curious
Fun web series for kids and parents exploring the birds and the bees
https://everybodycurious.com/

Health Powered Kids
Body Image and Self Esteem activities for kids
https://healthpoweredkids.org/lessons/self-esteem-and-body-image/

Kiddiematters
Self-esteem resources
https://www.kiddiematters.com/self-esteem-resources-kids-freebie/

National Association for Self Esteem
https://healthyselfesteem.org/

Pacer National Bullying Preventions Center
Information on bullying related issues
https://www.pacer.org/bullying/info/

Planned Parenthood Ask Roo
Free and private chatbot to answer awkward questions about sexual health
https://www.plannedparenthood.org/learn/roo-sexual-health-chatbot

Planned Parenthood Video
Video for parents helping them have tricky conversations in an open and positive manner.
https://www.youtube.com/watch?v=EinNeciMgpQ

Prevent Child Sexual Abuse
Resource for the prevention of child sexual abuse
https://www.preventchildabusenc.org/resource-hub/about-child-sexual-abuse/

Queer Kid Stuff
for kids and families to learn the ins and outs of the spectrum of gender identity and sexual attraction
https://www.queerkidstuff.com/

RespectAbility

Sexual education resource

https://www.respectability.org/resources/sexual-education-resources/

Stop Bullying

Information on bullying, cyberbullying, prevention, and response.

https://www.stopbullying.gov/

Stop It Now

Helping prevent sexual abuse in children

https://www.stopitnow.org/

1.888.PREVENT

Teen Help

Help for common adolescent development issues.

https://www.teenhelp.com/

TeenLine

Anonymous, nonjudgmental space for youth.

https://www.teenline.org/

800-852-8336

TeenTribe Wellness Community
Peer-to-peer support group for teens
https://support.therapytribe.com/teen-support-group/

The National Suicide Prevention Lifeline
Confidential support for people in distress
800-273-TALK (8255)

Trans Youth Equality Federation
Support for transgender youth and their families
http://www.transyouthequality.org/

TransYouth Family Allies (TYFA)
Support for transgender youth and their families
http://www.imatyfa.org/

The Trevor Project 24/7/365 Lifeline
Crisis Services for LGBTQ Young People
https://www.thetrevorproject.org/
866-4-U-TREVOR (866-488-7386)

Index

Printed in Great Britain
by Amazon

24414181R00059